P9-CQM-002

BIRD WORLD

Struan Reid

Consultant: Sylvia Sullivan

DORSET PRESS
NEW YORK

Series Editor: Julia Gorton
Editors: Heather Amery, Anne Civardi and Amanda O'Neill
Designers: Anita Ruddell and Hans Verkroost
Art Editor: Rowena Alsey
Picture Research: Lakshmi Hughes
Typesetter: Kerri Hinchon
Production: Sarah Schuman

Maps by Euromap Ltd

Cover illustration by Ken Lilly
Additional illustrations by John Francis/Bernard Thornton Artists

Published in 1991 by
Hamlyn Children's Books,
part of Reed International Books Ltd.,
Michelin House, 81 Fulham Road,
London SW3 6RB

© Reed International Books Limited 1991

All rights reserved. No part of this publication may be reproduced,
stored in a retrieval system, or transmitted, in any form or by any
means, electronic, mechanical, photocopying, recording or otherwise,
without the prior permission of copyright holders.

This edition published in the USA by Dorset Press, 1991
Dorset Press is a division of Marboro Books Corp.

Printed and bound in Hong Kong

ISBN 0-88029-694-1

Contents

All About Birds

There are about 8,600 species of birds in the world, ranging in size from tiny hummingbirds to huge ostriches. Apart from bats, birds are the only true flying vertebrates, or animals with backbones. They are also the only animals with feathers. Their whole bodies are especially designed for flight, with wings instead of front legs, or arms, and hollow bones to make them as light as possible.

Painted Bunting

Fine Feathers

Birds have different types of feathers for different jobs. They have soft, fluffy down feathers next to their skin to keep them warm, and "contour" feathers that cover their bodies and give them shape. Flight feathers are longer and tougher, with a strong central shaft. Many birds have feathers that blend in with their background and help them hide from their enemies. Some have brightly colored feathers to attract a mate.

An Old Bird

The first bird lived on the Earth about 150 million years ago. It was about the size of a crow and was called *Archaeopteryx*. It had wings and feathers, like a bird, but a lizard's head, with sharp teeth instead of a beak. Later, somewhere between 10 and 60 million years ago, true birds began to appear on the Earth.

Archaeopteryx

Out of the Egg

All birds lay eggs that hatch into baby birds. Some lay just one egg, others can lay four times their own weight in eggs. Many chicks are born blind, naked, and helpless. They depend on their parents for warmth and food while they grow. Others are covered with warm down, and are able to follow their parents soon after hatching.

Chick with Down

Bare Chick

During the dry season, queleas feed on small grass seeds picked up from the ground.

Red-billed Quelea

Tools of the Trade

The shape and size of a bird's beak depends on what it eats. Many birds that eat insects have long, slender beaks to catch and hold their tiny prey. Seed-eaters and nut-eaters have strong, short beaks, that are often curved, to break open their food. Birds that feed on nectar have long, thin beaks to probe deep into flowers. The powerful, hooked beaks of birds of prey are used to tear and cut meat. Fish-eaters have long, sharp bills that are often notched, with hooked tips.

Red-throated Bee-eater

Eastern Double-collared Sunbird

These brilliantly colored sunbirds feed on insects and the nectar of giant lobelias.

When this bee-eater catches a bee, it rubs it against a branch to get rid of its stinger, before swallowing it whole.

This bird spends hours walking over sunbaked mud or sandy soil looking for seeds to eat.

Chestnut-backed Finch Lark

Little Penguin

Water Wings

All birds have wings, but not all of them can fly. Penguins cannot fly through the air but they "fly" under the water. Using their short wings as flippers, they can reach speeds of over 25 mph (40 kph).

Sweet Melodies

Many birds sing songs to attract a mate and to drive away rivals. Their songs may be simple calls, such as a cuckoo's, or shrill melodies with hundreds of notes, like a wren's. Some birds can even sing two songs at once.

Skylark

How Birds Fly

Birds glide, soar, flap, or hover. The shape and size of their wings vary from species to species, depending on the birds' lifestyles, where they live, and what they eat. But all birds have strong, light, slightly rounded wings that act as natural airfoils, lifting them up into the air and keeping them aloft. They also use their wings to steer as they fly through the air.

How to Fly

Many birds fly by flapping their wings, using them just like oars. Strong downward beats of their wings lift the birds up into the air and drive them forward. This uses up a lot of energy. Some birds save energy by gliding, holding out their wings and riding on an airflow. Others soar on upward-moving air currents, hardly moving their wings.

Different Designs

Birds that fly very fast and need good steering, such as falcons and martins, have slender, curved wings that sweep backward. Short, broad wings allow forest birds to dodge between the trees and bushes. The long, narrow wings of an albatross are especially designed for gliding and soaring. Albatrosses may ride the wind for hours and hours, hardly ever moving their wings. But if there is no wind, they may not be able to fly at all.

Marginal Coverts

Primary Coverts

Secondary Coverts

Primary Flight Feathers (used for forward thrust)

Secondary Flight Feathers (used for uplift)

Alula (used to control airflow at low speeds)

A Thrush's Wing

Hovering High

All hummingbirds are masters at hovering. These tiny birds are able to beat their wings at a speed of up to 80 beats a second. They can hover at one spot without moving at all, especially as they suck nectar from flowers with their tubelike tongues.

Andean Hill Star Hovering

A Mallard in Flight

A Soft Landing

As a bird comes in to land, it spreads out its wings and tail to help it brake and land softly on the ground. It also spreads the alula, a small group of feathers at the front of its wings, to control the airflow over its wings. Then the bird swings its body upright to shift its weight toward its legs. Finally, it untucks its legs just before it meets the ground.

Whinchat Landing

Swift at Rest

Life on the Wing

Swifts spend their lives in the air. They feed and even bathe on the wing, flying in and out of the water. They can sleep in the air, still flapping their wings while they do so. Swifts only stop flying to nest and raise their young. They are helpless on land because their legs are too weak to stand on. But they can hang onto things with their feet.

Californian Condor Soaring

Soaring on the Wind

Large soaring birds, such as eagles and condors, have wide-spaced primary flight feathers. As they soar, they spread these feathers far apart. Each feather then acts as a separate tiny airfoil, giving extra lift. This helps hunters like the Californian condor make full use of every rising current of air.

In the Rain Forests

The steamy rain forests are found near the Equator, in parts of South America, Africa, and Southeast Asia, where the weather is very hot and wet. Because there is no cold season, plants in the rain forests can grow very quickly throughout the year in the hot, humid conditions. Thick creepers hang down from the trees in great curls and loops, with orchids and ferns growing from them. More types of plants, animals, and birds live in the world's rain forests than anywhere else.

There may be as many as 100 different kinds of trees in just one square mile of forest. They grow very tall, with smooth gray trunks and strong roots to support their great weight. They grow so close together that the branches and leaves at the top block out almost all the sunlight.

The rain forests are home to some of the most colorful birds on Earth. Many of them feed on the fruits, seeds, and nuts that grow on the trees. Others, such as the hummingbirds, sip nectar from flowers, and many more eat the huge insects that creep among the branches. Over the treetops, birds of prey, such as eagles and hawks, swoop down to catch smaller birds and monkeys.

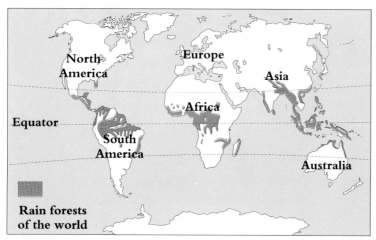

Rain forests
of the world

1 Crested Eagle
2 White-collared Swift
3 Hyacinthine Macaw
4 Short-billed Pigeon
5 Blue-throated Piping Guan
6 Squirrel Cuckoo
7 Rufous-browed Pepper-shrike
8 Ornate Umbrella Bird
9 Cayenne Jay
10 Black-eared Fairy
11 Silver-throated Tanager
12 Semicollared Hawk
13 Collared Forest Falcon
14 Fork-tailed Wood Nymph
15 Bronze-tailed Plumeleteer
16 Chestnut Woodpecker
17 Rufous-capped Spinetail
18 Great Jacamar
19 Black-throated Trogon
20 Cock of the Rock
21 Red-capped Cardinal
22 Brazilian Tanager
23 Band-tailed Barb-throat
24 Long-tailed Hermit
25 Red-billed Scythebill
26 Gray-winged Trumpeter
27 Marbled Wood Quail
28 Spectacled Owl
29 Black-bellied Gnateater
30 Gray-throated Leaf-scraper

Birds of the Rain Forests

The rain forests are very quiet places, although many different types of birds live in them, especially at the tops of the trees. The calls of birds sometimes ring out through the silence, but many birds are rarely seen because they are so shy.

Brilliantly colored birds, such as toucans and macaws, live in the top branches, where they eat seeds and fruit. Birds that live at ground level are often much duller in color. In the Amazon forest alone, there are more than 600 different kinds of birds.

African Green Pigeon

Plump Fruit-eater

African green pigeons have plump bodies but they can fly quickly through the forest trees looking for their favorite food, juicy, ripe figs. They will cover a large area in their search.

Blue and Yellow Macaw

Large Beaks

With their large, arched beaks, red-billed dwarf hornbills pluck figs, berries, and palm nuts from the forest trees. They then tip their food to the back of their throats and swallow it whole.

Red-billed Dwarf Hornbill

Carnival Colors

Blue and yellow macaws are brightly colored and noisy members of the parrot family. They fly around in pairs or in large flocks, squawking loudly. They eat a lot of fruit from the forest trees.

The macaws' favorite food is large, oily nuts, which are inside thick shells that they break open with their powerful beaks. Their beaks are so strong that the birds can hang from them or use them as an extra claw when climbing trees.

Buff-headed Wood Hoopoes

Gossiping Grub-eater

Buff-headed wood hoopoes are very noisy birds. Large groups of them chatter their way through the forest, as they search the bark for grubs and insects.

Speedy Hunter

Striped harpy eagles hover above the treetops and swoop down to prey on other birds, as well as mammals such as monkeys and sloths. They have short wings so that they can twist and turn through the trees at speeds up to 50 mph (80 kph).

Harpy Eagle

Jewel Colors

Angolan pittas are very colorful birds, known as "jewel thrushes." Although they can fly, they spend much of their time running around on the forest floor in search of beetles and other insects. If Angolan pittas are alarmed, they will sit down and fluff up their feathers.

Angolan Pitta

Secret Splendor

Very little is known about Congo peacocks. They were first seen in 1937, in the rain forests of eastern Congo in Africa. They are very shy birds and creep around quietly on the forest floor.

Congo peacocks were once hunted for their richly colored feathers, which were used to decorate headdresses.

Rain Forest Facts

Rain forests cover an area about the size of the United States. The largest is the Amazon forest in South America.

Nearly half the world's species of birds are found in the rain forests of South America.

It rains nearly every day in rain forests. At least 80 in (203 cm) falls each year, and sometimes as much as 150 in (381 cm). The forests are hot and damp all year round and the temperature rarely drops below 80°F (26.6°C).

The crest on top of a Congo peacock's head shows that it is related to the more familiar Asian blue peacock.

Congo peacocks may grow to a height of 26 in (66 cm).

Congo Peacock

11

Dazzling Feathers

The island of New Guinea is covered with high mountains and thick rain forest. Tropical fruits grow quickly in the hot, damp forests and there are vast swarms of insects. They provide plenty of food for some of the most colorful and amazing birds in the world.

The most brilliant of the New Guinea birds are the birds of paradise. Many of them are now close to extinction. This is partly because their habitat is being destroyed to make way for more farmland and also because they have been hunted for their feathers for many years.

King of Saxony Bird of Paradise

Greater Bird of Paradise

Long Plumes

Although a male King of Saxony bird of paradise is usually only about 7 in (18 cm) long, its beautiful head plumes can grow to 18 in (46 cm). The females of most types of bird of paradise are dull brown, gray, or green. This keeps them well camouflaged when nesting in the rain forest.

Wiry Feathers

Greater birds of paradise live in the lowland forests of New Guinea. Their lacy, elegant plumes may be 20 in (50 cm) long, while the two wiry feathers that hang down beneath the plumage may reach 30 in (76 cm).

Magnificent Riflebird

Flashes of Color

The magnificent riflebird climbs among treetops, eating fruit, spiders, and insects. In the shade of the trees, the male looks black, but in sunlight its feathers are a great flash of color.

Fancy Feathers

Victoria crowned pigeons are the largest pigeons of all, sometimes growing to a height of 33 in (84 cm). They feed on fallen fruit, and small groups of 5 to 10 will forage together on the ground. If they are disturbed, they fly up from the ground, landing heavily on nearby branches. This has always made them easy prey for hunters, who shot them for their feathers.

Victoria Crowned Pigeon

Princess Stephanie Bird of Paradise

Silky Tail

The Princess Stephanie bird of paradise lives in the dense forests of New Guinea's eastern highlands and feeds on fruits plucked from the tops of the trees. It is a very quiet bird, although when it flies, its tail feathers – which may be as long as 24 in (60 cm) – rustle like silk in the air.

Courtship Displays

All birds need to have young, or breed, so that their species will survive. To breed, male birds must attract females as mates. Many of the birds of New Guinea try to attract females by showing off, or displaying, their gorgeous plumage.

Victoria crowned pigeons (1) display by raising their crests and bowing gracefully. Magnificent riflebirds (2) and magnificent birds of paradise (4) stretch their heads up to show off their throat feathers. Acrobatic white-plumed birds of paradise (3) and raggiana birds of paradise (5) hang upside down, with their beautiful tail feathers spread wide.

1

2   3

4

5

In the Cold Forests

Vast forests of fir and pine trees stretch across the top of Europe, Asia, and North America. The trees are known as evergreens because they keep their leaves throughout the year. They are also called coniferous trees because they have cones.

These cold forests cover about 10 percent of the Earth's surface, but fewer birds are able to live in them than in the warmer woodlands farther south. The birds that stay all year round are mostly seed-eaters and birds of prey. Insect-eating birds are rare, and the few that visit the forests move on as soon as the insects disappear at the start of winter.

Cold forests of the world

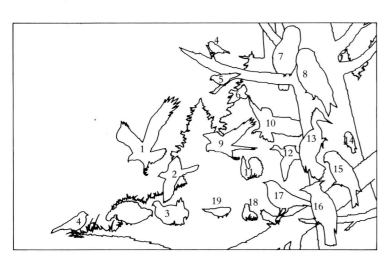

1 Fish Hawk
2 Siberian Jay
3 Black Grouse
4 Brambling
5 Pine Grosbeak
6 Tengmalm's Owl
7 Great Gray Owl
8 Ural Owl
9 Goshawk
10 Hawk Owl
11 Capercaillie
12 Goldeneye
13 Goosander
14 Siberian Tit
15 Crossbill
16 Waxwing
17 Siberian Ruby Throat
18 Hazel Hen
19 Nutcracker

Birds of the Cold Forests

Only a few kinds of birds can survive the bitterly cold winters of the northern forests. Those birds that do live there have adapted to the severe conditions. Most, such as finches and nutcrackers, feed on the seeds of the conifer trees that grow there. They have special beaks, strong enough to crack open the hard shells of the seeds. Every two or three years, the trees produce a lot of seeds. During these years, the number of birds increases. When there are fewer seeds, the birds fly south to find food.

Goshawk

Fearless Hunter
One of the boldest of all birds of prey, goshawks are not even afraid of people. They twist and dart through the dense forest, chasing after animals and birds.

Kirtland's Warbler

Rare Bird
Kirtland's warblers are among the rarest birds in America. There are fewer than 500 birds. This is because the young jack pine trees they live in are found in only one small area in Michigan.

Shy Singer
Townsend's solitaire is a very shy member of the thrush family. Like most thrushes, it sings beautifully. It feeds on the berries from juniper trees and sometimes catches insects in the air.

Townsend's Solitaire

Brambling

In Search of Insects
Bramblings live throughout the forests of Europe. In summer, they eat mainly beetles, caterpillars, wasps, and spiders. During the winter, they change their diet and feed mostly on seeds.

Cassin Finch

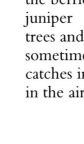

Mountain Finch
The Cassin finch is one of the most common birds along the Pacific coast of North America. In cold winters, the bird flies down from the cold forests to find food.

ller's

Boisterous Blue

With its handsome dark-blue feathers and high crest, Steller's jay is a noisy, busy bird. Its loud, harsh call cuts through the silence of the forest at the first sign of danger.

Strong Beaks

White-winged crossbills have very strong, crossed-over bills. They use these for breaking open hard pinecones to eat the seeds inside.

Cold Forest Facts

When food is hard to find in the cold forests of Asia, thousands of crossbills, nutcrackers, and waxwings invade the European woodlands farther south.

During the cold winter, spruce grouse survive by feeding almost entirely on conifer needles.

Most of the coniferous trees produce their seeds in woody cones, except yews and junipers, which have berries. These seeds provide food for many small birds.

Noisy Displays

Capercaillies are found only in the mountainous regions of Europe and the lowland forests of Siberia. To attract as many females to mate with as he can, the male bird performs a strange courtship display. He perches on top of a rock or tree, or on a patch of open ground, and sings, leaps in the air, and struts around.

During his courtship display, the male fluffs up his neck feathers and fans out his tail.

White-winged Crossbill

Spruce Grouse

Capercaillie

All Spruced Up

Spruce grouse are found in the huge coniferous forests that stretch across Canada and the northernmost parts of the United States. During the mating season, the males strut around and raise their tails to attract a female.

The male capercaillie is bigger than the female and may grow to be almost 3 ft (1 m) long.

17

The Cold Poles

The polar regions lie at the "top" and "bottom" of our planet. They are the coldest places on Earth. The North Pole lies in the middle of a huge frozen sea called the Arctic Ocean. The South Pole lies on the desolate, frozen continent of Antarctica. Although it is bitterly cold, the waters around it are full of tiny plants and animals, called plankton, which are a rich source of food for birds.

The lands around the Arctic Ocean are known as the tundra. During the winter, only a few species of birds can survive there, but in the short, warm summers, millions of birds fly up from the south to breed.

North America

Europe

Asia

Equator

Africa

South America

Australia

Polar regions of the world

1 Great Skua
2 Wilson's Petrel
3 Cape Pigeon
4 Black-browed Albatross
5 Sooty Albatross
6 Wandering Albatross
7 Broad-billed Prions
8 Giant Petrel
9 Sheathbill
10 Blue-eyed Cormorant
11 Dominican Gull
12 Gray-headed Albatross
13 Snow Petrel
14 King Penguin
15 Adélie Penguin

Birds of Antarctica

Most of the birds that breed in Antarctica are seabirds. They are usually bigger than land birds and better adapted to survive the freezing weather and terrible storms. For more than six months of the year, they feed at sea, on a plentiful variety of fish, squid, and plankton.

In the spring, flocks of gulls, cormorants, terns, and skuas return to the empty lands.

In the Antarctic, where spring begins in September, many birds make their nests among the stones and tough grass of the rocky islands that provide a little shelter and cover. Others lay their eggs on the ice and snow.

Wandering Albatross

Gray-headed Albatross

Albatrosses build their nests, which are big mounds of earth and grass, on windy slopes. They need a downward slope so that they can take off into the wind.

Majestic Wanderer

The wandering albatross is the world's largest seabird. It is a majestic flyer and can glide along for thousands of miles without flapping its huge, graceful wings. This magnificent bird feeds far out at sea. It sits on top of waves with its wings folded, waiting to pounce on a squid or other large sea creature on the surface.

Smaller Cousin

The gray-headed albatross is a smaller member of the albatross family, with a wingspan of about 6.5 ft (2 m). It has a long beak with sharp edges and a hooked tip for tearing slippery squid and fish. The female lays only one egg each season, in a nest of grass and mud. The chick is fed by its parents for about 30 weeks before it is left to fend for itself.

With the biggest wingspan of all birds, a wandering albatross can measure 12 ft (3.5 m) from wing tip to wing tip.

Nest Robbers

Great skuas nest on the islands and coasts of Antarctica. They have clawed feet and powerful, hooked beaks. Skuas raid the nesting sites of penguins, petrels, and other skuas, where they eat unguarded eggs, chicks, and even injured birds.

Greedy Feeders

Yellow-billed sheathbills are the only land birds that breed in Antarctica. They are very greedy and will often steal food from penguin chicks, eat penguin eggs, and even kill weak or injured birds. They spend most of their time running and hopping along the beaches looking for food.

Giant Petrel

Great Skua

Yellow-billed Sheathbill

Blue-eyed Cormorant

Messy Eaters

Blue-eyed cormorants nest on the cliffs, close to the sea where they feed. Their untidy nests are made of seaweed, feathers, and even bones, all stuck together with their droppings. The birds dive for fish and search the sea bed for shellfish and worms.

Oily Defense

Giant petrels lay their eggs in a stony nest. They hatch after eight or nine weeks. New giant petrel chicks are often attacked by skuas. They defend themselves by spitting out streams of red oily fluid.

Polar Facts

Glaciers move down the Antarctic mountains to the sea. There, blocks of ice break off and float away as icebergs.

In 1958, the U.S. submarine *Nautilus* was the first to go under the ice – a distance of 1,830 mi (2,945 km).

There is no land at the North Pole, only a huge mass of ice floating on the Arctic Ocean.

About two thirds of the Antarctic is covered with ice, over 1.2 mi (2 km) thick in places.

Arctic Homes and Summer Visitors

The Arctic tundra, a huge, flat, treeless expanse of land, stretches across the northern part of North America, Greenland, and northern Asia. There the dark winters are bitterly cold and thick snow covers the ground. During the short summers, it is light during the day and the night.

As soon as the snow melts in May and June, thousands of birds arrive to breed. Most have flown great distances from warmer climates. They leave again as soon as winter sets in. Only the toughest birds live in the tundra all through the year.

Bird Hunters

The gyrfalcon is the largest falcon in the world and lives all over the Arctic. Its favorite food is ptarmigan, which it snatches with its sharp talons, sometimes after a long chase. These falcons usually lay their eggs in the old nests of ravens or rough-legged buzzards.

Gyrfalcon

Big White Hunter

Snowy owls are one of the few birds that live in the Arctic all year round. They feed mainly on small mammals called lemmings. In good years, when there are lots of lemmings to eat, snowy owls lay up to 12 eggs. But when there are very few lemmings, snowy owls do not breed at all.

They build their nests on high ground so that they can watch out for any enemies. The females sit on the eggs, while the males find food and defend their families. Male snowy owls are almost completely white, while the larger females are white with black stripes.

Snowy Owl

Like most owls, they have good sight and very good hearing.

Snowy owls fly slowly, hardly making any noise.

Snowy owls have thick feathers on their feet to help keep them warm.

Redpoll

Food Under the Snow

Tiny redpolls survive the Arctic winter by squeezing underneath the snow cover to search for food.

A Change of Color

During the winter, snow-white ptarmigans are protected from the cold by their thick feathers. In the summer, they become darker, which helps camouflage them from their greatest enemy, the gyrfalcon.

Peregrine Falcon

Black Raider

Ravens are big, noisy members of the crow family. They survive in the Arctic by eating anything they can find. Many live near human settlements, where they raid garbage dumps for food. Because they are so adaptable, ravens can survive in all sorts of different places throughout the world.

Steep Dive

Peregrine falcons live in many different habitats, including the Arctic tundra. One of the largest falcons, they may grow to 19 in (48 cm) long.

Peregrine falcons feed mainly on other birds and small animals. When hunting, they fly high up into the sky, then turn and dive down onto their prey, reaching speeds of over 105 mph (170 kph). They often snatch smaller birds from the air in this way.

Raven

Summer Visitors

Each summer these birds, and many thousands of others, arrive from different countries all around the world to build their nests and lay their eggs in the Arctic tundra.

Because the summer is so short, the birds raise their chicks very quickly. In the Arctic, they store fat in their bodies to use on their return trip in August.

Dunlin

Turnstone

Long-tailed Duck

Knot

Brent Goose

Nesting on the Ice

Millions of penguins make their nests in the Antarctic and the rocky islands around it. Of the 18 different kinds of penguins, only three types of penguins lay their eggs on the ice.

Penguins cannot fly and can only waddle clumsily when on land. But they can swim very well, using their wings like flippers to "fly" through the water and leap onto the shore.

The birds have small, oily feathers with warm down underneath and a thick layer of body fat. This keeps the penguins warm in the icy waters and protects them from being battered by the rough waves when they land on rocky island shores.

Penguins feed in the sea, chasing after fish and diving down for squid and crabs and other food in the ocean waters.

Chinstrap

Little Chinstrap

The smallest penguin, it gets its name from its markings. It nests in huge colonies on Antarctic islands, the females laying one or two eggs.

Penguin Nurseries

King penguins leave their chicks while they go off to feed in the sea. The thousands of chicks huddle together in groups to keep warm. A few adults stay to guard them.

King

Emperors are the largest penguins, at about 3 ft (1 m) tall.

Emperor

The Emperors

At the start of winter, when the sea begins to freeze, emperor penguins return to Antarctica. Each female lays one egg and goes back to the sea.

The male penguin stands on the ice for two months in the dark winter without eating. He carries the egg on his feet, keeping it warm under a special flap of feathers.

When the chick hatches, the female returns to look after it and the hungry male goes off to feed.

Both parents feed their offspring by swallowing food themselves, and then bringing it up again into the chick's mouth.

Jackass

Rudder Feet

Jackass penguins use their webbed feet like rudders to steer under water. Their sleek waterproof feathers act as wet suits as they speed through the sea. They can swim as fast as 25 mph (40 kph).

Black and White

All penguins are black and white, and some have yellow markings and bright feathers on their necks.

These birds all live south of the Equator. They spend most of their lives at sea, coming ashore to breed and molt (lose their old feathers and grow new ones) in huge separate colonies. The thousands of penguins may look alike to us but most pairs meet again each year at the same site to make a nest and lay eggs.

Magellanic

Royal

Rockhopper

Erect-crested

Snares Islands

Macaroni

Galápagos

Peruvian

Yellow-eyed

Southern Gentoo

Death in the Sea

Adélie penguins are the favorite food of leopard seals, who lurk underwater, waiting for the penguins to jump in.

Leopard Seal Chasing an Adélie

Every year, in September and October, thousands of Adélie penguins go back to the Antarctic after spending the winter months far out at sea. Using the sun to guide them, they return to the same nesting places, sometimes walking up to 60 mi (100 km) across rough sea ice.

They often find their old nests of pebbles and stones, even when they are hidden by snow. The female usually lays two eggs, which hatch after 35 days. Nine weeks later, the chicks are ready to go to sea.

Adélie Parents with Their Egg

The Deserts

Most deserts are burning hot places during the day but at night the temperatures can fall to below freezing. The Sahara desert, in northern Africa, is the world's largest desert. It covers an area of more than 3 million sq mi (8 million sq km), making it bigger than Australia.

All deserts are very dry places with very little rain or even none at all. Few people can live in them but plants, animals, and birds survive the heat and lack of water, even in the harshest deserts. Most of the desert birds have pale, sand-colored feathers that help them to blend with their surroundings where there is little vegetation to hide in.

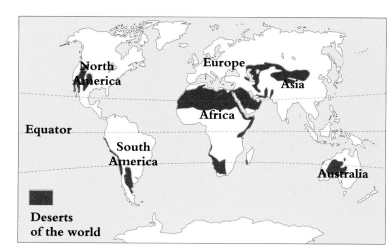

Deserts of the world

1 Houbara Bustard
2 Bar-tailed Desert Lark
3 Pratincole
4 Pallas's Sandgrouse
5 Brown-necked Raven
6 Stone Curlew
7 Egyptian Vulture
8 Steppe Eagle
9 Lanner Falcon
10 Desert Wheatear
11 Lesser Gray Shrike
12 Cream Courser

Birds of the Deserts

Many birds that live in deserts hide in the shade of rocks and plants during the heat of the day. Some small birds find burrows or dig holes to shelter underground from the sun. Because of their feathers, birds cannot sweat to cool down but some pant to lower their body temperatures. Birds that can glide spend the hot days soaring 3,000 ft (1,000 m) up over the desert, where the air is cooler.

Some desert birds live quite close to water holes but many are able to live without drinking water at all. They get the moisture they need from their food.

Dive Bomber

Lanner falcons are large birds of prey. They live in southwestern Asia and Africa. As well as catching their prey on the wing, they also swoop down in a steep dive and pluck it off the ground. Although they are usually found in the desert, many have moved to towns and cities.

Lanner Falcon

Sprinting Cuckoo

Roadrunners are members of the cuckoo family and live in the deserts of Texas and Mexico. Although they can fly, they prefer to dash around, grabbing birds' eggs and chicks, snakes, and lizards.

Roadrunner

Grass Dweller

Striated grass-wrens live in Australia. They have very squeaky calls and build their nests at the top of clumps of a spiky grass called spinifex.

Striated Grass-wren

Mystery Bird

Night parrots of Australia are so rarely seen that some people believe they are extinct. Very little is known about them. Although they can fly well, they prefer to stay on the ground. If they are disturbed, they run away rather than fly.

Night Parrot

Prickly Nest

The gila woodpecker nests in the tall, prickly cacti that grow in the California deserts.

Gila Woodpecker

Strutting Dandy

The rufous-crowned emu wren is the lightest and one of the shyest of all Australian birds. Its striking tail is made up of "filaments" like those of an emu.

Rufous-crowned Emu Wren

The Water-carrier

Lichtenstein's sandgrouse have a very clever way of carrying water to their chicks, sometimes over 20 mi (30 km). The male fluffs up his breast feathers and sits in the water. The feathers soak up water like a sponge. He then flies back to the chicks, which drink the water.

Elf Owl

Poorwill

Winter Hibernation

Poorwills live in the deserts of California. They come out at night and flutter around the bushes like giant moths. They are one of the very few birds known to hibernate in winter.

Tiny Hunter

Elf owls live in the deserts of the southwestern United States and Mexico. They are the smallest of all the owls. Despite their size, they will sometimes catch other small birds to add to their diet of grubs and insects.

Houbara bustards may grow to a height of 28 in (70 cm).

Lichtenstein's Sandgrouse

Striking Stripes

Houbara bustards are well camouflaged against the desert landscape when they are feeding or resting. But as soon as they open their wings to fly, they show bold black and white stripes. These birds use this striking display during courtship, when males spread out their wings and tail and raise their long black and white neck feathers.

Mourning Dove

Milk-fed Young

Mourning doves live all over North America. They fly in small flocks, feeding on seeds from bushes. They can survive without water longer than most birds.

Mourning doves feed their young with "pigeon milk." This is a food that both parents make in their throats.

Houbara Bustard

Houbara bustards do not need to drink. They get enough water to live on from insects and desert plants.

Desert Facts

Gila woodpeckers make their nests in holes of the saguaro cactus. This helps to strengthen, not damage, the cacti. The birds act as tree "surgeons," often digging out damaged or diseased parts of the plant for their nest holes.

Roadrunners sprint on their long sturdy legs at a steady speed of 15 mph (24 kph). They run in straight lines and also zigzag between plants and stones. Under pressure, these birds, which are the size of chickens, can run at 25 mph (40 kph).

The Wetlands

The streams, marshes, and lakes that lie inland, the rivers that wind their way to the sea coasts, and the shallow shorelines are homes to millions of birds. These areas are rich in plant and insect life that attracts the birds to feed and breed. They are found all over the world, from the cold, boggy lands of the north to the hot tropical swamps.

The birds that live there come in all shapes and sizes. Some have long legs to walk in shallow water, long beaks to probe for food in the mud, or webbed feet to paddle across the water. Some birds float on the waves, diving for fish and underwater plants.

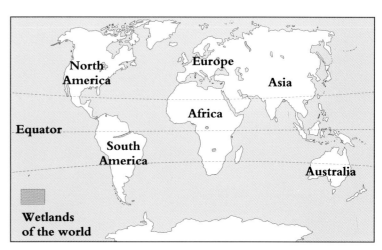

Wetlands of the world

1 Giant Kingfisher	**12** Hammerhead
2 Malachite Kingfisher	**13** Black Crake
3 Common Snipe	**14** Anhinga
4 African Black-crowned Crane	**15** Sacred Ibis
5 Shoebill	**16** Stanley Crane
6 Stork	**17** Black-winged Stilt
7 Pangani	**18** Greater Flamingo
8 Purple Gallinule	**19** African Spoonbill
9 Pink-backed Pelican	**20** Gray Heron
10 White Pelican	**21** Egyptian Goose
11 Lesser Flamingo	**22** African Finfoot
	23 Great-crested Grebe

Lakes, Rivers, and Streams

Great numbers of birds come to feed and live on rivers and lakes. A river may start as a mountain stream of icy water. By the time it reaches the sea, it has grown much broader, and the water flows more slowly. As the river changes, so do the types of birds that live on its banks.

The slow-moving rivers and deep, still lakes are full of fish. The banks are thickly covered with grasses, bushes, and trees. The many insects attract a wide variety of birds.

Spoonbill

Spooning Its Food
When it is feeding, a spoonbill walks through shallow water, gathering up small plants with its strange bill.

A Life-long Bond
Sarus cranes are among the largest cranes in the world. They mate for life and their partnerships are so strong that they are always together.

Sarus Crane

Deep Feeder
The exceptionally long legs of a black-winged stilt allow it to go out looking for food in much deeper water than most other birds.

Black-winged Stilt

Long Toes
Pheasant-tailed jacanas are known as "lily-trotters." They have long legs and very long toes that spread their weight. They trot across the water by stepping on the plants. The females are larger than the males, and can be very aggressive.

Pheasant-tailed Jacana

Hoatzin

Mute Swan

Black Swan

Beautiful but Fierce

Mute swans are large birds with long, graceful necks. They build huge nests from piles of reeds on the riverbanks or on islands. The males will always defend their nests, hissing and beating their wings to drive out any intruder.

Killed for Its Color

Because its feathers are black with only a little white on the edges of its wings, people used to think that the black swan lived with the devil. Because of this, many were killed in Europe, where it was introduced from Australia.

Tree Climber

The hoatzin is a strange member of the cuckoo family. It lives near the Amazon and Orinoco rivers in South America, although only the hoatzin chick can swim. Sometimes it eats so many leaves that its throat becomes heavy and it has to rest it against a tree branch. It has claws on its wings, which it uses to climb up trees.

Lesser Flamingo

Gray Wagtail

Common Sandpiper

Pink Filter Feeders

Thousands of lesser flamingoes gather on the huge soda lakes that run along the Great Rift Valley in Africa. The salty water is full of microscopic plants called algae. This is the only source of food for these birds. They suck up the water into their bills and then force it out again, filtering out the algae as they do so.

Stream Feeders

Gray wagtails usually live near mountain streams. The rushing water is full of the bugs and grubs that the birds feed on.

Winter Traveler

Common sandpipers can often be seen feeding in shallow water. They travel from Europe to Africa in winter, using the same routes year after year.

Swamps and Marshes

Swamps and marshes are strange places, half water and half land. They are rich in many different plants, fish, small animals, and minerals, attracting thousands of different water birds to feed and breed. There are two types of marsh and swampland, freshwater and saltwater. Freshwater marshes and swamps are usually found around lakes or ponds, or beside rivers. Saltwater marshes are along coastlines, often where rivers join the sea.

White with Age

A young bald eagle keeps its brown feathers until it is seven years old. Then it grows bright white head and tail feathers, which slowly appear after each molt. Pesticides on farmland have reduced numbers so much that this huge bird is now protected by law.

Bald Eagle

Shoebill

Hammerhead

Upstairs and Downstairs

A hammerhead builds its huge nest with three "rooms." It lays its eggs in the top room, the chicks move to the middle room after they have hatched, and the bottom room is an "entrance hall."

Ruff

Shoebills

Shoebills get their names from their huge bills, which look like wooden shoes. They hunt by standing with their wings open to drive the fish into shallow water, where they can catch them.

All Ruffed Up

Each spring, male ruffs gather for a "meeting," where they dance in front of each other and defend their territories.

Snake Birds

Darters are also known as snake birds because they swim through the water with only their heads and long necks showing, looking like wriggling snakes. They spear fish with their pointed bills, toss them up in the air and then swallow them. The birds' necks bulge as the fish pass down into their stomachs.

Darter

Roseate Spoonbill

Scarlet with Age
When they are young, scarlet ibises have dull-colored feathers. The bright red adult plumage grows over a number of years, and gets stronger as the bird gets older.

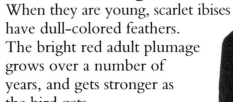

Scarlet Ibis

Night Fisher
The beaks of spoonbill chicks look like those of any other baby bird. As the chicks grow, their beaks grow longer, and develop a bulb at the end. By the time the chick leaves the nest, the beak looks like that of an adult bird. Spoonbills feed by touch, so they are able to feed at nighttime, when most other birds are asleep.

Great blue herons can grow over 4 ft (1.2 m) tall.

Great Blue Heron

Mandarin Duck

Herons have a harsh, rasping cry.

Gaudy Tree-nester
Most ducks spend their days on the water, and nest on the ground close by. Some, such as mandarin ducks, perch in trees. They build their nests in hollows in the trees, high up above the ground. The males are very colorful, while the females are quite plain.

Wetland Facts

Large, colorful snails in the Everglade swamps of Florida are eaten by some of the birds that live there, such as the limpkin and the Everglade kite. Drainage and other factors have reduced the numbers of snails. This has, in turn, affected the number of birds in the area.

The largest nest ever recorded was built by a bald eagle in the Everglades. It was 20 ft (6 m) deep, 9.5 ft (2.9 m) wide, and weighed over 2 tons.

Powder Puffs
Like all herons, great blue herons have special feathers for grooming that break up into powder. They have one "powder puff" on their chest, and two on each thigh. Herons clean off the slime from fish by rubbing their head and neck feathers through the powder puffs, and then combing off the sticky balls with one of the claws on each foot.

Skilled fishers, great blue herons stand very still in the water, patiently waiting for fish.

At the Sea's Edge

Huge colonies of birds nest on the rugged sea cliffs. Some places, such as the island of St. Kilda off the coast of Britain, are home to many millions of seabirds. In winter, the cliffs are buffeted by gale-force winds, and by huge sea waves.

In the summer months, the cracks, crevices, and narrow ledges of the sea cliffs are smothered with great numbers of breeding birds. They fill every available space on the rock faces, and feed on the rich stocks of fish swimming in the water below.

Paddle Power

The common diving petrel dives into the sea, using its short wings like paddles to swim underwater. It then bursts out of the water, often with a fish in its beak.

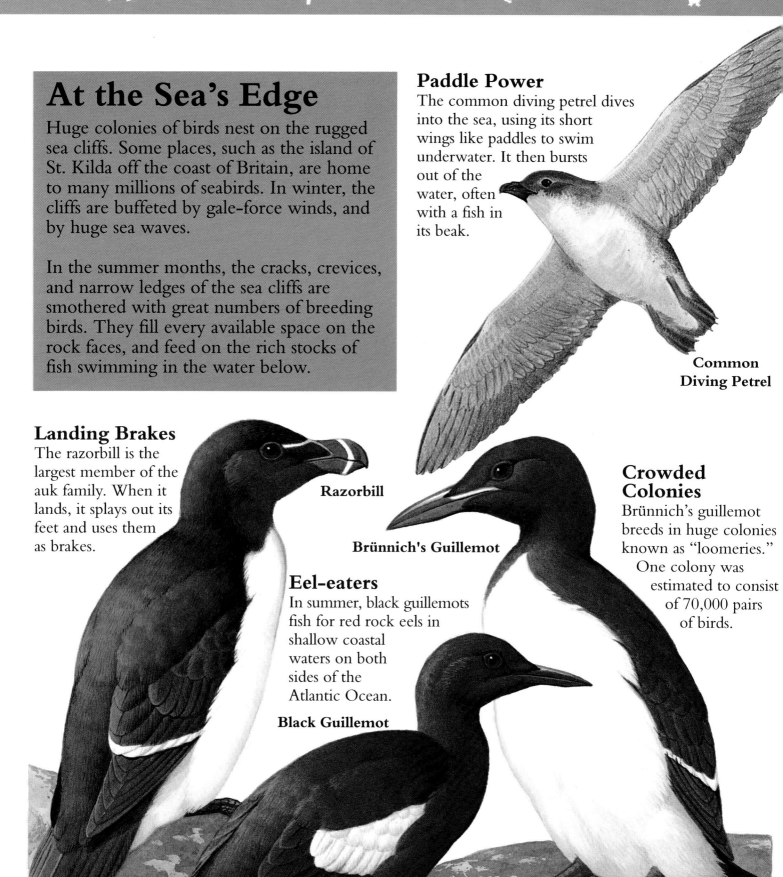

Common Diving Petrel

Landing Brakes

The razorbill is the largest member of the auk family. When it lands, it splays out its feet and uses them as brakes.

Razorbill

Brünnich's Guillemot

Eel-eaters

In summer, black guillemots fish for red rock eels in shallow coastal waters on both sides of the Atlantic Ocean.

Black Guillemot

Crowded Colonies

Brünnich's guillemot breeds in huge colonies known as "loomeries." One colony was estimated to consist of 70,000 pairs of birds.

Beaks for Food

Over thousands of years, seabirds have evolved different kinds of beaks to feed along mudflats and beaches. Many different types of birds can feed in the same places without competition, as they search for different foods.

With long, slender beaks, some birds probe deep into mud to catch burrowing creatures, such as worms. Those with short beaks pick food from the rocks and the top of mud and sand. Some birds have powerful beaks that can crush shells, while others have beaks that can prize open shells and pick out the flesh. Other birds eat grasses and seaweed, and many more feed on the fish in the sea.

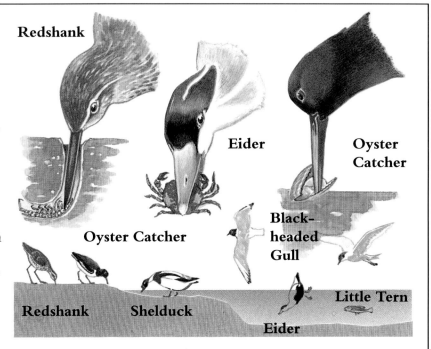

Redshank

Eider

Oyster Catcher

Oyster Catcher

Black-headed Gull

Redshank

Shelduck

Little Tern

Eider

Shelduck

Borrowing Burrows

Living among the sand dunes of a beach, shelducks build their nests in abandoned rabbit burrows. They can lay up to 16 eggs at a time. Soon after they hatch, the chicks are led to the water by their mothers.

Herring Gull

Bright Beaks

Once a year, after they have mated, puffins change their beaks. Their beaks are colored red, yellow, and blue for the breeding season to attract a partner. But after mating they shed the outer layer, leaving a dull-colored, smaller beak for the remainder of the year.

Dump Scavengers

Herring gulls pick up clams and crabs on the seashore and drop them from a height to break the shells. They also fly inland to feed from garbage dumps.

Puffin

The Woodlands

Broadleaf woodlands grow in the world's temperate zones, between the hot tropics and the frozen Poles. Broadleaf trees shed their leaves in autumn as protection against winter frosts.

Much of western and central Europe was once covered by one great forest of broadleaf trees. Over the centuries, much of the forest has been cut down and replaced with towns, villages, and farmland. Today, most of Europe's woodlands remain only in small stretches. They provide shelter for a rich variety of birds, which find food and make their nests in the trees and on the ground.

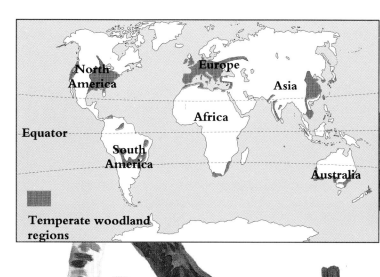

Temperate woodland regions

1 Tree Creeper
2 Blackcap
3 Yellowhammer
4 Willow Warbler
5 Hawfinch
6 Redstart
7 Sparrow
8 Wood Pigeon
9 Jay
10 Marsh Tit
11 Blue Tit
12 Robin
13 Nightingale
14 Sparrowhawk
15 Tawny Owl
16 Songthrush
17 Great Spotted Woodpecker
18 Green Woodpecker
19 Chaffinch
20 Nuthatch
21 Spotted Flycatcher
22 Pied Flycatcher

Birds of the Woodlands

Different kinds of birds live at different levels of the woodland. Some live in the top layer, or canopy, where the branches of the highest trees reach the sunlight. Other birds live in the shade of the forest floor. They feed on grasses and seeds or hunt for insects on the soil or among the fallen leaves.

The middle layer of the woodland is made up of shrubs, bushes, and smaller trees. It is rich in food for birds, from buds and berries to grubs and beetles.

A wide variety of birds find their food, make their nests, and raise their chicks in the different layers of woodland.

Red-shouldered Hawk

A woodpecker's neck and skull are specially developed so that they can take the shock of frequent hammering.

Woodland Hunter

The red-shouldered hawk of eastern North America perches in low trees and scans the ground for frogs, snakes, and mice.

Gaudy Glutton

Jays are one of the noisiest and most brightly colored of woodland birds. They eat almost anything, from fruit and buds to young birds.

Common Jay

Wood Borer

Woodpeckers have keen hearing to help them find insects under tree bark. They use their powerful beaks to drill into the tree trunks. Then they spear the insects with their special long, barbed tongues, and pull them out.

Great Spotted Woodpecker

The woodpecker's strong tail helps support it when pecking at a tree trunk.

Willow Warbler

Ground Nester

A shy songbird, the willow warbler lives in the lower layer of the woodlands and builds its domed nest of grass on the ground. In the autumn, it leaves Europe to spend the winter in Africa and returns in early spring.

40

Turkey

Saved from Extinction
European settlers almost wiped out the wild turkeys in much of North America. Game-control laws now protect them.

Red-headed Woodpecker

Halfhearted Migrant
Blackcaps feed, nest, and sing in the middle layer of the woodlands or on the higher branches. Here they may raise two broods of chicks each year. Many blackcaps migrate to North Africa for the winter but some stay in western Europe all through the year.

Blackcap

Smart Squabbler
Red-headed woodpeckers live in noisy, quarrelsome groups. Clearings made by tree felling attract these colorful birds.

Woodland Facts

It may take a woodpecker several weeks to bore out its nest hole in a tree.

Many woodland birds are probably more common today than when forests covered the land. They now live in clearings and newly planted woods. Woodland birds of prey need to be especially agile to dodge between branches as they hunt.

The woods of Tennessee and North Carolina have more types of trees than the whole of Europe.

Probing Beak
Woodcocks live in the damp forests of Europe and are well suited to life on the ground. Their brown feathers help them hide in the shade of the forest floor, and they use their long beaks to probe for worms in the damp earth and leaves.

Woodcock

Nutcracker
The European hawfinch has one of the strongest beaks of the bird world. With this, it can crack open the hardest seeds.

Hawfinch

On the Mountains

On a mountainside, different plants and trees grow at different levels. This is because the weather changes all the way up. At the foot of a mountain, it is often quite warm with plenty of rain and there are thick forests. Higher up, the air becomes cooler and drier. The forests give way to pine and fir trees, which live in the colder temperatures.

Higher still it becomes too cold even for trees and only small plants and shrubs grow on grassy slopes. At the top, there may be ice and snow all year round. Each different type of bird lives at the level of the mountain where it can find the food it needs.

1 Flame-crowned Tanager
2 Black-eared Golden Tanager
3 Andean Flicker
4 Tapacolo
5 Cock of the Rock
6 Horned Coot
7 James's Flamingo
8 Andean Condor
9 Mountain Caracara
10 Andean Hill Star
11 Barbet Toucan
12 Torrent Duck
13 Andean Swordbill
14 Ground Tyrant
15 Long-billed Starthroat
16 Purple-crowned Fairy
17 Masked Flower-piercer

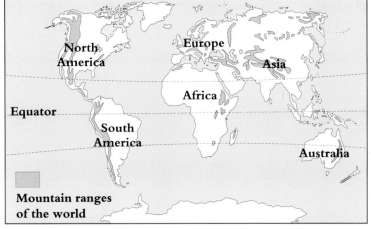

Mountain ranges of the world

42

Birds of the Mountains

Many different types of birds live on the world's mountains, from the ranges in the warm tropics to those in the colder areas. The birds vary according to which part of the world and where on the mountains they live.

Some birds build their nests in the bitterly cold areas near the tops of mountains. Others feed beside mountain lakes and streams, and still more live in the forests that grow on warm, lower slopes.

View to a Kill

Using the wind currents, the magnificent golden eagle can stay up in the air for many hours without coming down to rest. It circles slowly around, scanning the ground for animals to eat.

Andean Flicker

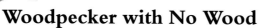

Woodpecker with No Wood

Although Andean flickers are woodpeckers, they live very high up on the sides of mountains where there are no trees. They build nests in tunnels dug into riverbanks, which shelter the young chicks from the cold and the fierce winds. The birds live in flocks of up to 30. They search the grass and stones for beetles and moth larvae.

Golden Eagle

Downhill All the Way

A Himalayan monal is a plump bird with a very loud call. When disturbed, it crashes around in the bushes, making a lot of noise. This makes it an easy target for hunters, and many thousands have been killed. To escape from attackers, it takes off and glides downhill. It then has to waddle all the way up again when danger has passed.

Elegant Loner

A spotted forktail hops daintily among the stones in a stream, searching for insects. It prefers to be on its own and, when it is resting, it sits quietly on a branch, waving its tail slowly up and down.

Rocky Camouflage

The snow finch is one of the most attractive mountain birds. When it is flying, its dazzling white plumage is easy to see. On the ground, its gray back helps camouflage it among the rocks.

Spotted Forktail

Snow Finch

Himalayan Monal

White-throated Swift

Aerial Acrobat

The white-throated swift is one of the fastest North American birds. It flies down mountainsides at great speed in search of insects. Like all swifts, it has weak legs that make it very clumsy on the ground.

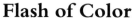

Andean Hill Star

High Hummingbird

Andean hill stars live very high up on mountains. To save energy on cold nights, their body temperature drops to that of the air. Like other hummingbirds, they suck nectar from flowers, but they also eat insects.

Flash of Color

An eastern double-collared sunbird is brilliantly colored. It sips nectar from flowers and eats insects. It lives high up in the mountains of Africa, in a remote area of cold mists.

Eastern Double-collared Sunbird

Mountain Facts

Birds of prey have the best eyesight of all birds. In the right conditions, a golden eagle can see a hare 2 mi (3.2 km) away.

Swifts spend nearly all their lives in the air. They eat, drink, and even sleep while flying.

Few birds live near the tops of the highest mountains in the Himalayas because weather conditions are so harsh and food supply so limited. But alpine choughs and lammergeiers have been seen above 26,000 ft (8,000 m).

Bone Breaker

One of the largest and most spectacular vultures, the lammergeier is also known as the "bone breaker." It drops animal bones from a great height onto rocks, and then swoops down to feed on the bone marrow. It also eats tortoises, breaking the shells in the same way.

Lammergeiers may have a wingspan of almost 9 ft (2.7 m).

Lammergeiers make their nests with sticks, bones, and animal skins.

Lammergeier

On the Grasslands

The grasslands are great plains that stretch to the horizon like a rolling sea of grass. They are found all over the world, wherever there is enough rain for grass to grow but not enough to support trees. Grasslands may be tropical, like the African savanna, or bleak and windswept like the Asian steppes.

The prairie grasslands of central North America stretch for thousands of miles. The prairie birds nest on the open ground. Many of them follow the grazing herds of deer, bison, and cattle, feeding on the insects disturbed by the animals' hooves.

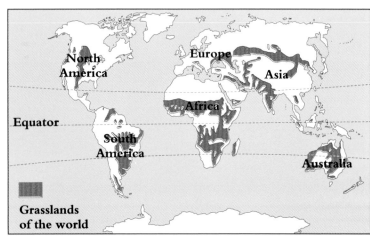

1 Rough-legged Hawk
2 Burrowing Owl
3 Whooping Crane
4 Canada Goose
5 Sage Grouse
6 Sharp-tailed Grouse
7 Greater Prairie Chicken
8 Prairie Falcon
9 Eskimo Curlew
10 Killdeer
11 Chestnut-collared Longspur
12 Bobolink
13 Brown-headed Cowbird
14 Western Meadowlark
15 California Quail
16 Lark Bunting

Grasslands of the world

Birds of the Grasslands

Many grassland birds spend much of their lives on the ground. The rolling plains offer few hiding places for predators, so the ground is a safe place.

Other birds spend much of their time in the air. Because there are no trees, songbirds cannot find perches from which to sing. Grassland birds, such as larks, sing during flight, high in the air. Hunting birds, such as falcons, use the air for spectacular courtship displays, diving from great heights.

Burrowing Owl

Short-toed Eagle

Snake Snatcher
Although the short-toed eagle of Asia will catch small rodents, lizards, or even large insects, it specializes in snakes. Its strong, stubby toes are specially adapted to grasp a wriggling snake.

Keen-eyed Hunter
A prairie falcon flies along at about 300 ft (100 m) above the North American prairies, searching with its keen eyes for small animals and birds on the ground. It drops on its prey so swiftly that it may tumble head over heels on the ground if it misses its target.

Prairie Falcon

Secretary Bird

Feathered Mole
The small burrowing owl, found in both North and South America, keeps its eggs and chicks safe by nesting underground in the abandoned holes of prairie dogs and other animals. It may even dig its own burrow in soft soil.

A Bird with a Kick
The secretary bird gets its name from its crest feathers, which look like old-fashioned quill pens. It strides across the African savanna in search of snakes, which it kills with powerful kicks of its long legs.

Crested Seriema

Reluctant Flier
The South American crested seriema lives on the ground, hunting insects, snails, and worms. When danger threatens, it is more likely to run away than to fly.

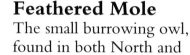

Steppe Eagle

Ground Nester
Although eagles usually nest in trees or on rocky crags, a steppe eagle will nest on the open ground. Its ability to adapt has helped make it the most numerous small eagle in the world. It is found in the grasslands of Africa and Arabia, as well as India.

Flightless Giants
Some grassland birds cannot fly and depend on size and speed for safety. They include the rhea of South America and the ostrich of Africa. The ostrich is the world's biggest bird, up to 9 ft (2.7 m) high, while the greater rhea stands 5 ft (1.5 m) tall. They can see danger from far away and are strong enough to fight off most attackers.

These birds can also run at great speeds, faster than a galloping horse. They live in large groups, often with herds of grazing animals. Both ostrich and rhea males are good fathers, making nests and sitting on the eggs.

Greater Rhea

Grassland Facts
Swarms of locusts and grasshoppers provide a feast for birds, such as the steppe eagles.

Many grassland birds follow grazing animals. Oxpeckers even ride on them, pecking ticks and flies from their skin.

Although the steppes of Central Asia seem bleak and unfriendly, they are rich in birdlife, with nearly 250 species.

The ovenbirds of South America build mud nests shaped like clay ovens.

Ostriches sometimes swallow stones to help them digest leaves and seeds.

Ostrich

Handsome white plumes are harvested by ostrich farmers in South Africa. Ostrich eggs are the largest eggs in the world. They may be 6 in (15 cm) long and 5 in (13 cm) wide.

Threatened Chicken
Once common in the North American grasslands, prairie chickens have been wiped out in many States. This is because of the plowing up of the grasslands by farmers and hunting.

Greater Prairie Chicken

Grassland Birds of Australia

Australia's grasslands stretch over 3 million sq mi (8 million sq km). They are harsh lands with little rainfall. Only grasses and a few tough trees, such as acacias and gum trees, can grow there. Yet many birds have learned to live in these dry grasslands. The water holes attract huge flocks of brightly colored parrots, budgerigars, and finches, sometimes in their millions. Giant flightless emus run through the grass like the ostriches of Africa. There are also strange birds called kookaburras, a type of kingfisher, which hunt insects, mice, and snakes in the dry grass.

Wedgetailed Eagle

King of the Skies
One of the largest eagles in the world, the wedgetailed eagle has a wingspan of almost 8 ft (2.5 m). It feeds on rabbits and other animals, and is strong enough to carry off a small wallaby.

Kookaburra

Showhouses and Gardens
Most male bower birds build complicated "showhouses," or bowers, to attract a mate. They decorate them with colorful feathers, flowers, shells, and leaves, and even paint them with charcoal and berry juice.

Some clear a small garden and display a collection of bright objects. Others build mounds, or huts, with avenues of sticks and grass leading into them.

Bower of Spotted Bower Bird

Spotted Bower Bird

Wild Laughter
Kookaburras are also called "laughing jackasses" because of their loud, laughing call, which echoes across the grasslands.

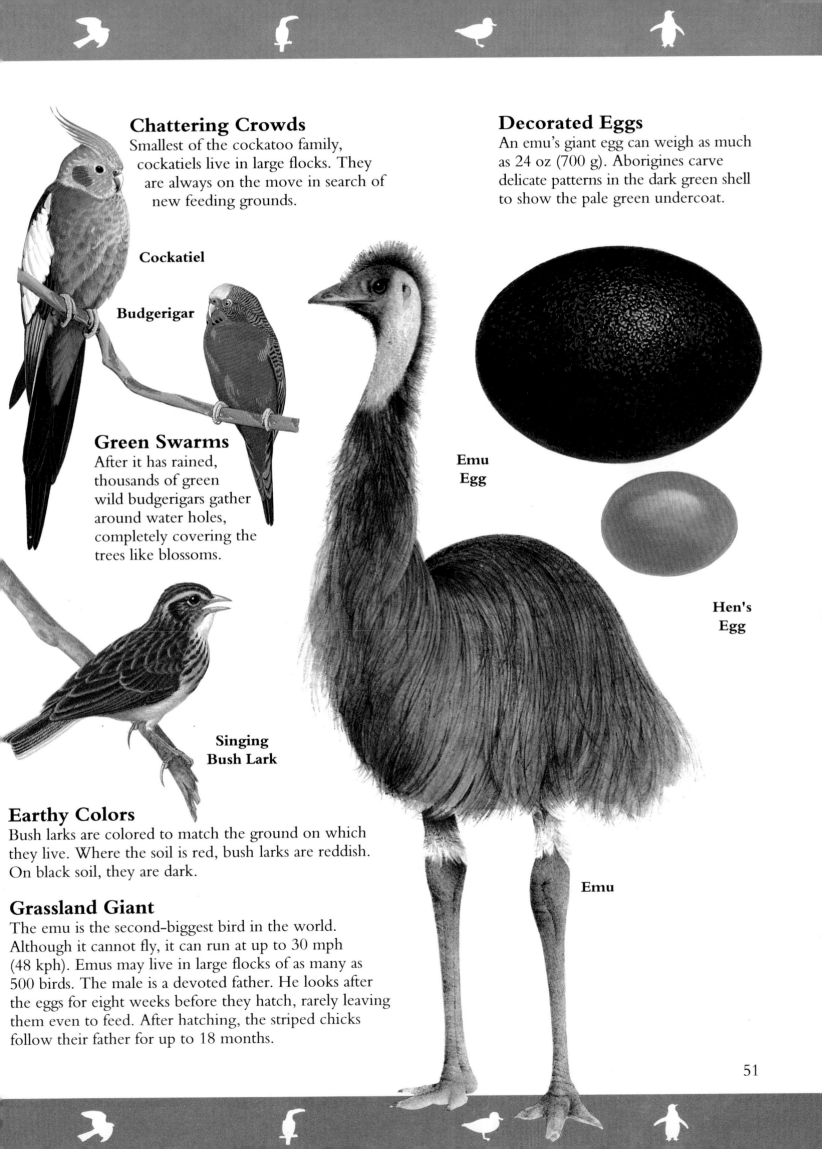

Chattering Crowds
Smallest of the cockatoo family, cockatiels live in large flocks. They are always on the move in search of new feeding grounds.

Cockatiel

Budgerigar

Green Swarms
After it has rained, thousands of green wild budgerigars gather around water holes, completely covering the trees like blossoms.

Singing Bush Lark

Earthy Colors
Bush larks are colored to match the ground on which they live. Where the soil is red, bush larks are reddish. On black soil, they are dark.

Grassland Giant
The emu is the second-biggest bird in the world. Although it cannot fly, it can run at up to 30 mph (48 kph). Emus may live in large flocks of as many as 500 birds. The male is a devoted father. He looks after the eggs for eight weeks before they hatch, rarely leaving them even to feed. After hatching, the striped chicks follow their father for up to 18 months.

Decorated Eggs
An emu's giant egg can weigh as much as 24 oz (700 g). Aborigines carve delicate patterns in the dark green shell to show the pale green undercoat.

Emu Egg

Hen's Egg

Emu

Hidden Homes

Although they prefer open spaces, barn owls will live in farm buildings and in towns, as long as open land is nearby for hunting.

Night Birds

When the sun goes down and night begins to fall, a great change takes place in the bird world. Most of the creatures that have been active during the day go to sleep, but others come out to hunt for food. These animals are nocturnal. Because it is difficult to see at night, the eyes of many nocturnal birds are extra large to help them find their way around in the darkness.

Little Owl

Stay-at-home

Because the little owl will eat whatever is available, it can stay in one place throughout the year.

Tawny Owl

A Change of Diet

In the countryside, tawny owls eat mostly small mammals, especially mice and voles. But when they live in towns, they eat small birds because there are fewer mammals to hunt.

Hawk Owl

Survival of the Fittest

The hawk owl gets its name from its long tail and swooping flight, which make it look like a hawk. Some years, when an owl cannot find enough food for all its chicks, the oldest and biggest chicks eat all the food. Then only one or two of the chicks survive.

Good Hearing

All owls have excellent hearing. Their ears are large slits on either side of a disk of feathers that surround their faces. These feather disks may also reflect noises into the owls' ears. In many owls, such as the barn owl, one ear is bigger than the other and it often grows lower down. These differences in size and position make it easier for the owl to figure out where a noise is coming from. Then it can swoop down and catch its prey in the darkness.

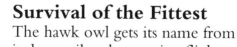

**Owlet
Nightjar**

Smelling for Food

Brown kiwis have nostrils at the very tip of their long beaks. Unlike most birds, which use sight and sound to find their food, kiwis use their sense of smell to hunt for insects and worms. They also have very sensitive bristles at the base of their beaks that help them find their way through the dark forest.

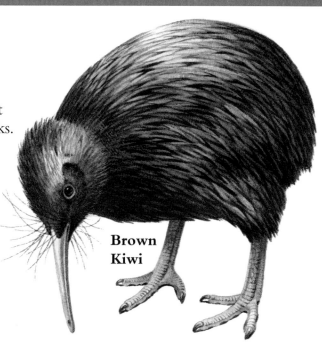

**Brown
Kiwi**

All-around Vision

At night, when an insect flies past, an owlet nightjar may jump up from its perch and catch it in its beak. The owlet's huge eyes are positioned so that it can see above its head without looking up.

**Tawny
Frogmouth**

Pennant-winged Nightjar

Broken Branches

If it is disturbed, a tawny frogmouth points its head upward and closes its eyes to make itself look like a broken branch.

Flag Feathers

Pennant-winged nightjars are the largest of the African nightjars. In the breeding season, the males grow long flight feathers, up to 2 ft (60 cm) long, which they keep until after they have mated.

Scooping it Up

Boat-billed herons use their strange-looking broad bills to scoop up small fish and shrimps. During the day, they rest quietly among the grasses and trees.

Boat-billed Heron

Barn Owl Flying with Mouse

Feathered Friends

Some species of birds have adapted to life in cities and towns after having their natural habitats destroyed by human beings. They nest and feed in parks and gardens and often make their homes on tall buildings. Some small birds, such as house martins, build their nests under the eaves of houses, while others nest high up on the ledges and windowsills of apartment buildings. In winter, when small birds may freeze to death, cities provide warmth and plenty of food. The birds feed on waste from garbage cans and on scraps of food left out for them on bird feeders.

Superb Blue Wren

Courting Colors

Superb blue wrens are a common sight in the town gardens of southeastern Australia. During the breeding season, they are usually seen in pairs or in groups of six or seven. In each group there is only one brightly colored male. The other males are more like the females, with drab brown feathers.

Blue Jay

Magpie Lark

City Dweller

The Australian magpie lark has adapted easily to city life, feeding on insects in garden lawns. A fierce defender of its territory, it will even attack its own reflection in a window, or the hubcap of a car.

Bird-feeder Bully

One of North America's best-known birds, blue jays live in crowded towns and cities. They often bully other birds and rob their nests. Like other types of jays, they are quick to grab food, and swoop boldly down to eat scraps left out on bird feeders. Despite their beauty, blue jays are not very popular because they often drive other birds away from parks and gardens.

Not a Robin

The American robin is not a true robin. It is really a large thrush. But like the European robin, it has made its home in towns and cities, nesting in yards and feeding tamely on lawns. The robin builds itself a big cup-shaped nest made of mud, twigs, and grasses. It lays four to five eggs up to three times each breeding season. In late summer, when there are more robins about, they feed on fruits and insects.

American Robin

Owl About Town

Many owls, such as the great horned owl of America and the tawny owl of Europe, have left the woodlands to live in cities. These tawny owls have changed their diet from small mammals to mainly sparrows and starlings.

Tawny Owl

Great Horned Owl

House Martin

Sitting Tenants

Many species of birds, such as blackbirds, house sparrows, blue tits, chaffinches, and doves have become a familiar part of city and town life. Each year, especially in winter, these birds rely on people for food and shelter. In turn, many city people welcome them, luring them to their gardens with scraps of food, water, birdhouses, and bird feeders filled with seeds and nuts. Birdbaths attract birds both to drink and to bathe. Garden trees and bushes make natural nesting sites, but many birds prefer to use the warm and cosy birdhouses.

Collared Dove

Blackbird

House Sparrow

Chaffinch

Blue Tit

Building Nests

Most birds build nests to keep their eggs safe and warm, and to rear their young. They may be simple hollows in the ground, elaborate nests of twigs and grass, or huge mounds of earth. Eagles build vast nests of sticks and twigs. Some come back to the same nest each year and add more branches. African sociable weaverbirds work together to build a nest for up to 300 pairs of birds. But not all birds build nests. Emperor penguins carry their eggs on their feet, under a flap of skin to keep them warm.

A Foster Home

Cuckoos lay their eggs in other birds' nests. The baby cuckoo hatches before the other eggs and pushes them all out of the nest. The foster-parents feed the greedy chick, which may grow much bigger than they.

Reed Warbler

Cuckoo

Sedge Warbler

Bearded Tit   **Reed Bunting**

Living Pebbles

Birds that nest in open fields or on the seashore have nowhere safe to build their nests. Instead, they lay their eggs on the bare ground. Many of the eggs are marked with streaks and blotches to match the earth and stones where they are laid. The eggs look just like pebbles and are well-camouflaged against predators. When the chicks hatch, they are covered with speckled down so that they can hide among the pebbles.

Nesting in the Reeds

The tall, dense reeds and marshland grasses make a safe home for many kinds of birds. Water birds, such as moorhens, build a floating raft at the edge of the water, moored to the reeds. Other birds make their nests among the reeds themselves. Some nest at ground level, where thick stems hide their eggs and young. Here the bearded tit builds its rough, untidy nest of grass and reeds. Songbirds, such as sedge warblers and reed buntings, hang their nests up in the reeds. A reed warbler weaves its deep, cone-shaped nest halfway up the tall reed stems, where it is hidden from enemies both from above and from below.

Tailor-bird

Sewing a Nest

To make its amazing nest, a tailor-bird sews two leaves together. He uses his beak as a needle to make holes in the leaves, and uses strands of cobweb for thread. Then he lines the tiny nest with fine grass and down to make it warm for the eggs.

Weaving a Nest

Weaverbirds live in large, noisy flocks, and may build as many as 40 nests in the same tree. Male weaverbirds weave grasses or rushes together to make strong hanging nests.

Female weaverbirds lay their eggs at the top of the nest, at the end of a long tunnel, to keep them safe from predators.

Weaverbird

Cup Nest

Small birds that live in trees or shrubs often make an open, cup-shaped nest. The chaffinch weaves its nest from grass, roots, moss, and cobwebs. It adds a soft, thick lining of hair and feathers to keep its eggs warm.

Chaffinch

Hornbill

Treetop Fortress

Hornbills build their nests inside hollow tree trunks. To keep the eggs safe from hungry monkeys and snakes, the male seals the female in. He blocks the entrance with mud, leaving a small slit to pass food through to her. She chips her way out when her babies are big enough to fend for themselves.

Great Travelers

Many birds breed in parts of the world where the winters are too harsh for them to survive. Every year, many leave their breeding grounds and fly to warmer places, often thousands of miles away, where it is easier to find food. A few months later, at the beginning of spring, they make the long journey back home to nest again. This year-by-year traveling is called migration.

Many birds find their way back to the same nesting place year after year. How they do it is still a mystery. They may use the stars and sun as guides. Landmarks, such as mountains, valleys, and rivers may also help them. Even very young birds seem to know where and when to go.

Great Shearwater

Ospre

Sedge Warbler

Nonstop Flyer

Most migrating birds fly at night, stopping during the day to rest and feed. But the sedge warbler makes its journey from Europe to Africa in four days and nights without stopping.

A Long, Windy Journey

Adult great shearwaters leave their breeding grounds a week or two ahead of their chicks. Helped by strong following winds, their long migration journey may take more than nine months. In late April, they leave the southern Atlantic Ocean, where they breed, and fly northward. The whole of their journey is spent at sea, feeding on fish and squid as they travel.

Broad-winged Hawk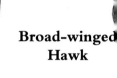

Main Flight Paths

The migration journeys that many birds make each year can be very dangerous. Sometimes the wind blows the birds off course, food is hard to find, and predators lie in wait. Birds choose the most direct and least dangerous routes to fly.

The three main migration routes of the world avoid the Atlantic and Pacific oceans and the most dangerous mountains and deserts of Eurasia and Africa.

Main Flight Paths

Sharp-shinned Hawk

Marsh Hawk

Rough-legged Buzzard

Red-shouldered Hawk

Red-tailed Hawk

Bald Eagle

Golden Eagle

Turkey Vulture

Easy Pickings

Many birds of prey lie in wait, ready to pounce on the migrating birds as they fly past. The tired birds make easy pickings for hungry hunters, such as gabar goshawks, lanner falcons, sooty falcons, and Eleanora's falcons.

Eleanora's Falcon

Gabar Goshawk

Over the Mountains

To help them travel faster, some birds use the strong, upward air currents that blow over high mountains. Every year, thousands of birds migrate along the Appalachian mountains in the United States.

Globetrotters

Arctic terns make the longest migration journey of all birds. They fly from their breeding grounds near the Arctic Circle all the way to Antarctica, almost 13,000 mi (21,000 km).

Arctic Tern

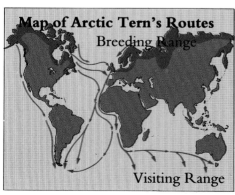

Map of Arctic Tern's Routes
Breeding Range

Visiting Range

Birds in Danger

All birds can breed and raise their young when the conditions where they live are right. If their habitats are threatened—the trees cut down, the land cleared, or their food poisoned by agricultural insecticides and pesticides—they cannot breed successfully. All over the world, there are many types of birds in danger of dying out.

Souvenirs

Quetzals of South America are hunted for their beautiful feathers, which are sold as souvenirs to tourists.

Quetzal

Great Indian Hornbill

Rare Woodpecker

There are probably no ivory-billed woodpeckers left in the swamps of Louisiana, although some have recently been discovered in Cuba. The bird's disappearance from its Louisiana home has been caused by tree clearance.

Hunted

Great Indian hornbills may grow as long as 4 ft (1.2 m). Many of these birds have been hunted and killed for their meat.

Saved from Extinction

Flightless takahes of New Zealand were thought to be extinct 40 years ago. Some live birds were then discovered in a remote valley, and now about 250 of them survive. It was partly because of hunting that their numbers dropped so low.

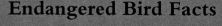

Ivory-billed Woodpecker

Endangered Bird Facts

At Loch Garten, Scotland, rare ospreys are protected by a 24-hour watch while they are nesting.

Hawaiian geese, once in danger of becoming extinct, were taken from the wild and protected in zoos. Their numbers have recovered, and several hundred have been released back on their island home.

Most of the remaining Spanish imperial eagles are protected in the Coto Doñana reserve in Spain.

Takahe

Californian Condor

Mountain Vulture

So many Californian condors have been hunted and killed that there are now very few birds left. If attempts to breed these birds in captivity are not successful, they will become extinct.

Spanish Imperial Eagle

Emperor of the Skies

Only about 100 pairs of Spanish imperial eagles survive. As well as being hunted, their homes have been destroyed and their food poisoned.

Survivors

Noisy scrubbirds were thought to be extinct, until some were found living in southwestern Australia in 1961. Although much of the woodland where these shy insect-eaters live is being drained and cleared for building, their numbers now seem to be increasing.

Noisy Scrub-bird

Walking Before Flying

Although ground parrots are good fliers, they spend much of the time walking on the ground. Their numbers have been affected by the clearance of the thick bushes in Australia, where they make their homes.

Ground Parrot

Captured and Caged

Parrots make very colorful pets, and they are often captured to be sold as cage birds. A lot of these birds are caught in West Africa, which is home to many different types, from the talkative African gray to the green-yellow Senegal. More than 75 percent of the parrots captured there are sent to the U.S. and Europe. Birds such as cockatoos are taken young, when they are still in their nests.

African Gray Parrot

They then begin a journey of many thousands of miles. For every bird that completes the trip, ten die of shock during capture or from being kept in terrible conditions with little food.

Senegal Parrot

Competition for Food

The rare grass-eating Cape Barren goose lives on a few islands off the coast of Australia. It has to compete for its food with the thousands of sheep that have been imported and now live on the islands. Many of the geese have been shot by the sheep farmers.

Cape Barren Goose

Penguin at the Equator

Small Galápagos penguins live much farther north than the rest of the penguin family. Pollution and hunting by people who steal their eggs have reduced their numbers.

Galápagos Penguin

61

Glossary

Adapt To change to fit in with new surroundings.

Antarctic Area around the South Pole. Also called Antarctica.

Arctic Area around the North Pole.

Bird of Prey A bird that feeds on other animals.

Camouflage Coloring or patterns on feathers that help birds match their surroundings.

Canopy The rooflike cover made by the treetops in a forest or wood.

Carrion The meat of dead animals.

Climate The type of weather in a given region.

Colonizer A bird that settles in a new place to live and breed.

Colony A group of the same type of birds nesting together in one place.

Coniferous A tree, usually with needlelike leaves, which keeps them all year round.

Courtship The way a male bird behaves to attract a female to breed with and produce young.

Deciduous A tree that loses its leaves at the end of the summer.

Display The way a male bird shows off his feathers, preens, dances, or flies to attract a mate, or to defend his territory.

Endangered Species A type of bird that is in danger of dying out.

Environment The surroundings in which a bird lives.

Evolve To change and develop slowly, over thousands or millions of years.

Extinct A type of bird that once lived on the Earth, but has now died out.

Flock A group of the same type of birds.

Hibernation A long, deep sleep, or time of little activity, during cold or heat, or when there is no food.

Hover When a bird beats its wings and stays motionless in the air.

Incubate When a bird sits on its eggs to keep them warm, so that the chicks inside can grow and develop properly.

Migration A regular journey made by birds, often at a certain season, to avoid a cold winter, a drought, to find food, or to breed.

Molt The time when a bird loses its old feathers and grows new ones.

Nocturnal Active at night.

Pampas The grasslands of South America.

Plankton Tiny, floating plants and animals that drift on the surface of the sea or lakes.

Plumage A bird's feathers.

Poles The most northerly and southerly places on Earth.

Prairie The grasslands of North America.

Predator A bird that kills other birds or animals for food.

Prey A bird or animal that is killed by another animal for food.

Preening When a bird cleans, tidies, and oils its feathers with its beak.

Primitive An early form of bird.

Rain Forest A dense forest of tall trees found in tropical regions.

Savanna The grasslands of Africa.

Scavenger A bird that eats dead animals or plants, or the remains of another predator's kill.

Species A particular type of bird within a family group.

Steppe The grasslands of Europe and Asia.

Taiga Coniferous forests stretching across northern Europe and Asia.

Talon A bird's sharp, hooked claw, used to catch and grip its prey.

Tundra Frozen, treeless land between the North Pole and the northern forests.

Vegetation Plant life, including trees, shrubs, grasses, and flowers.

Vertebrate An animal with a backbone, such as a bird or mammal.

Wingspan The distance between the tips of a bird's spread-out wings.

Index